Original title:
Golden Waters

Copyright © 2025 Creative Arts Management OÜ
All rights reserved.

Author: Evelyn Hartman
ISBN HARDBACK: 978-1-80581-618-8
ISBN PAPERBACK: 978-1-80581-145-9
ISBN EBOOK: 978-1-80581-618-8

Sunlit Dreams Along the Riverbank

In the sun, fish dance and sway,
A turtle steals my sandwich today.
I chase a duck; it quacks in glee,
While I trip on roots—oh, dear me!

Splashing water in a good old fight,
My friends all cheer; it feels so right.
We float on tubes, though one is torn,
A leak, oh no! I'm now forlorn.

Dragonflies twirl; I try to catch,
But they giggle, dodging like a match.
A frog jumps high, and what a show,
I laugh so hard, my drink will flow.

As daylight fades, we share our tales,
Of splashes made and fishy fails.
With laughter loud, our hearts will sing,
Sweet summer memories—oh, what a fling!

Reflections of a Shimmering Heart

A mirror pond where frogs take heed,
They croak and boast; it's quite the breed.
I glance in, see my goofy grin,
As dragonflies buzz—let the fun begin!

I toss a pebble with a splash,
My dog jumps in! My heart takes a bash.
He paddles proud, but oh, what a sight,
A soggy pup, he's quite the fright.

Sunset glimmers on the water's face,
I try to dance—oh, what a disgrace!
I trip and fall with a comedic grace,
The fish, they chuckle; I'm losing my place.

Floating leaves, they spin and twirl,
I muse aloud, "Is life a whirl?"
With every laugh, the ripples break,
In shimmering hearts, joy is the takeaway!

Shimmering Reflections

In puddles deep, the ducks do skate,
Reflecting faces, isn't that great?
A fish does wave with a flippy fin,
While a cat just ponders where to begin.

A splashy dance, the children cheer,
As soggy socks bring on good cheer.
The sun's bright grin, a cheeky sight,
Bouncing rays give everyone a fright!

Liquid Sunlight

A lemonade stand, oh what a show,
With straws like rays that come and go.
The pitcher's bright, it brings such cheer,
But sips too big cause a lemonade smear!

It sparkles and giggles, mimics the sky,
As ice cubes jingle with a sly little sigh.
A bumblebee tries to take a sip,
And lands right in, oh what a trip!

The Alchemy of Light

With sparkles bright, the sunlight bends,
While fish in shades do twists and wends.
A water sprite with a chuckle sings,
While juggling flasks and shiny things!

A splash of hue, a pop of glee,
Turns tadpoles into frogs with a tea party spree.
They leap and croak, all sounds galore,
In this bizarre aquatic folklore!

Glistening Tides

The ocean laughs, it tickles toes,
Each wave a giggle, but who really knows?
Seagulls mock with their cheeky squawks,
While crabs do dance in their little frocks.

A jellyfish floats like a soft balloon,
Comedic art in the light of the moon.
The tide rolls in with a playful shove,
A splashy hug from the sea we love!

The Art of Flowing Light

A jellyfish waltzes with grace,
Bubbles giggle, floating in space.
Crabs wear suits made of seaweed,
They toast with shells, 'Here's the deed!'

Seagulls squawk out a funny tune,
While fish ignite like a bright balloon.
The ocean laughs in rippling waves,
As clams join in with their silly raves.

Caresses of the Sunlit Sea

The tide tickles toes with a splash,
While dolphins play, making a dash.
A starfish strikes a pose, quite bold,
As sandcastles crumble, stories told.

Seashells giggle at tales abound,
On sandy shores where fun is found.
Each wave arrives with a playful cheer,
Whispering secrets for all to hear.

Flickers of Celestial Emotions

Starfish worn like royal crowns,
Make doodles giggle, flip me upside down.
A shrimp jumps high with a giant grin,
While lobsters dance, calling me in.

Moonbeams sparkle on the laughing tides,
Where sea turtles wear surfboards like rides.
The night hosts a party, bright and grand,
With jellyshots made of ocean sand.

The Horizon's Radiant Touch

A line where sea hugs the sky,
Clouds wear shades, waving goodbye.
Waves crack jokes, rise, and fall,
As sunbeams wander, free for all.

A pelican slides in with a splash,
Chasing the tide like a merry dash.
The boats are waving flags of cheer,
On this wild ride, nothing to fear.

The Whispering Wavelengths

In a stream where jokes arise,
Fish tell tales to the skies.
A turtle cracks a witty grin,
While ducks take bets on who'll win.

The frogs in suits swim by with flair,
They ponder life and fashion wear.
The sunbeams laugh, they tickle the waves,
As bubbles float like merry knaves.

Celestial Reflections

Stars peek down to take a dip,
With giggles from a comet's trip.
A moonbeam splashes on the cheek,
While stardust dances, quite unique.

Planets roll and have a ball,
They trip on moons and then they sprawl.
"Who knew we'd have such fun," they sigh,
As shooting stars go zooming by.

The Dance of Amber Ripples

Ripples laugh and twist with glee,
A dance-off for all to see.
The little fish with sparkly tails,
Are busting moves; there's no need for scales.

The seahorses join in the fray,
With the crabs doing the funky sway.
They spin and twirl in shimmery light,
While coral bursts into silly delight.

Embrace of the Luminous Cascade

Waterfalls giggle as they glide,
Wrestling rainbows by their side.
Bubbles play tag, no need to see,
As whirlpools shout, "Come dance with me!"

The rocks chuckle, their edges worn,
Try to paint the grasses, all adorned.
With splashes and flips, they make a splash,
In this cascade of joy, they dash!

The Spectacle of Dawn

As the sun peeks, fish start to dance,
They wiggle with glee, in watery prance.
Under the surface, seaweed jokes flow,
While clams crack up, putting on quite a show.

A splashing otter, wearing a grin,
Snaps selfies with turtles, much to their chagrin.
Giggles and bubbles, a waterway fair,
Where laughter is caught in the salty air.

Radiant Rivulets

Through the meadows, a shimmering trail,
With ducks in tuxedos, no need to regale.
They quack out tunes as they paddle along,
While frogs join the chorus with their ribbiting song.

Bubbles rise up, it's a bubbly parade,
The fish flaunt their scales, never afraid.
Straw hats on turtles, a sight to behold,
In this watery world, there's laughter untold.

The Embrace of Saffron Streams

Bouncing through shallows, a hare takes a dip,
He swims like a pro, but can't quite flip.
With friends all around, they chuckle and glide,
As villagers watch from the riverbank side.

Jellybeans float by, a spectacular sight,
The frogs have a party, oh what pure delight!
With each splash of cheer, they relish the scene,
In the embrace of this stream, life is serene.

Celestial Waters

Stars twinkle down, in a splashy display,
As raccoons dunk cookies, in an absurd way.
They fish for sweet treats, with winks and a grin,
While the otters hold hands, and attempt to spin.

The moon shimmers bright, making shadows that dance,
With frogs practicing moves, all caught in a trance.
As laughter erupts, in this vibrant expanse,
The night's full of whimsy, a watery romance.

Secrets Beneath Shimmering Skies

Frogs in tuxedos, hopping with glee,
Making splashes, that's their decree.
Under the moonlight, they'd dance and prance,
While fish in bow ties just join the romance.

Crabs flip their claws like they're in a band,
Playing on shells, isn't it grand?
Each ripple a giggle, each splash a delight,
The sea's full of secrets, hiding in light.

The Gift of Glistening Tides

Seagulls are swooping, stealing my fries,
With a wink and a nod, oh what a surprise!
The tide rolls in, with a bubbling cheer,
As dolphins wear hats, oh give them a beer!

Octopuses juggling, with pearls all around,
Their circus is wild, hilariously crowned.
Each wave a chuckle, each crest a grin,
In this liquid laughter, we all join in.

Luminous Legacies of the Deep

The fish tell tales that make you snort,
Of underwater battles and a big old sport.
A crab in a shell claims to be a knight,
Only to trip over his own tail in fright!

Mermaids in bubbles are having a ball,
Splashing and singing, they're loving it all.
With laughter as bright as the stars up above,
The ocean's their playground, their home full of love.

Vessels of Sun-Spun Serenity

Sailboats are swaying like they're in a trance,
While jellyfish waltz in a shimmering dance.
The sun winks down, giving fish some flair,
As turtles in sneakers just glide through the air!

A wave makes a joke that's safe for all ears,
While seaweed giggles, tickling fears.
In this watery world, we all have a say,
Where laughter is current and silliness waves.

The Secret Life of Sparkling Currents

Under the bridge, a fish wears shades,
Proudly flaunting its trendy parade.
With bubbles popping like fizzy drinks,
It swims in rhythm, what fun it thinks!

A turtle dabs on sunscreen galore,
Sips kelp smoothies by the river shore.
The ducks are giggling in a neat row,
While the frogs sing hits we all know!

Chasing Glints on the River's Face

A squirrel dives for a shiny snack,
But the fish just splashes, making a crack.
They play tag under the beaming light,
While the crabs cheer, oh what a sight!

The sunbeam dances with shadows near,
Waving to all with a chuckle and cheer.
In every ripple, a story is told,
Of laughter and antics, pure and bold!

Shimmers of a Dreaming Sea

The seagull squawks with a feathered flair,
While a clam just stares, pretending not to care.
A jellyfish boogies with graceful moves,
While the starfish mimics, grooving in grooves!

Shells play poker, they bluff and they fold,
The octopus giggles, oh what a bold!
Each wave a chuckle, each splash a cheer,
In underwater hilarity, they disappear!

The Symphony of Shining Waves

Waves clap like fans at a comical show,
As seaweed sways to and fro, oh so slow.
Crabs don tuxedos, with bows on their back,
While the fish cartwheel on their slippery track!

Anemones bloom in extravagant style,
Each petal sways, making the day worthwhile.
The ocean erupts in a bubbly spree,
As laughter and joy dance wild and free!

The Tidal Glow

The waves like jelly, start to jig,
Splashing around, a blurry pig,
Crabs doing dance, no time to spare,
They twist and twirl without a care.

A seagull squawks, a wacky joke,
While clams are plotting— oh, they spoke!
The sun's a grill; the sand, a fry,
Sandy toes wave to the sky.

Picnic ants in mosh pit throng,
Seeking crumbs to keep them strong.
A beach ball bounces, takes a dive,
Chasing it, a toddler strives.

As night draws near, stars shine so bright,
Whilst mermaids giggle, just out of sight.
Every splash, a laugh, a cheer,
The tidal glow brings fun all year!

Reveries on the Shining Banks

The banks are paved with shiny dreams,
Where fish wear hats, or so it seems.
A frog croaks jokes, a stand-up star,
While turtles race in a game bizarre.

Picnickers fight with sandwich mice,
As ants debate on who's too nice.
Fishes play tag beneath the waves,
Synchronized swimming? That's how they rave!

A pelican drops a soda pop,
And everyone laughs when it goes plop.
Crabs in tuxedos sashay with grace,
In this strange, silly, watery place.

As twilight falls, the giggles rise,
Reflections dance in the evening skies.
With every ripple, laughter spills,
On these bright banks, joy surely thrills!

Sunkissed Cascades

The waterfalls shimmer like buttercream,
Where ducks in shades plot to scheme.
They paddle in lines, like a school parade,
Each quack a giggle, plans remade.

Splashes that tickle from head to toe,
As kids play pirates, yelling, "Whoa!"
With rubber ducks afloat like boats,
While squirrels eye snacks with sly little quotes.

Bubbles are dancing, glimmering light,
As the frogs host a concert tonight.
They croak in chorus, the beat is fine,
With the fish as the fans, dancing in line.

Beneath the sun, the laughter flows,
In a world where silliness truly glows.
The cascades shimmer with a laughter spree,
In this zany dream, we all feel free!

Serene Reflections of the Day

The sun bows down, the sky's a peach,
Where turtles whisper and crabs teach.
They hold a class, "How to Chill", it's true,
While I just watch, not knowing what to do.

As shadows drift, the laughter plays,
With shiny fish in their bright displays.
They flash their scales, like disco lights,
While the snails race, bringing us delights.

Old boots and driftwood make a smile,
As I trample over them once in a while.
Birds wearing hats drop breadcrumbs with flair,
The whole day's a riot and I'm just aware!

Reflections shimmer in a giggly haze,
Where every moment offers a joyful gaze.
The day winds down, but don't dismay,
In this happy realm, we'll always stay!

Luminous Currents

The fish are wearing sun hats, oh so bright,
They throw a party, dancing in the light.
Crabs play tunes on seashells with glee,
While the frogs croak jokes, sipping on tea.

A turtle brings cake, it's a wobbly ride,
With sprinkles and icing, they eat side by side.
The ducks quack rhymes, it's a sight to behold,
While the water shimmers, like liquid gold!

Mirror of the Dusk

Reflections ripple, giggles in the frame,
Fish wearing sunglasses, it's all a game.
The frogs jump high, try to touch the moon,
While the snail's slow dance is a funny tune.

The dragonflies gossip, buzzing all around,
With rumors of frogs that never get found.
The sky paints colors, a wild delight,
As all the critters party into the night.

Harvesting Daydreams

A scarecrow dreams of an irrigation dance,
While pumpkins sing ballads, oh what a chance!
But the corn keeps laughing, it might just pop,
As the sun rolls in for a lazy drop.

The farmers wear socks that clash with their boots,
And the chickens are plotting to steal their fruits.
With laughter and soil, they make quite the scene,
In a harvest of giggles, a whimsical dream.

The River's Gilded Path

The ducks are playing poker on a log,
While otters slide by, they jest and they hog.
The beavers are busy, with wagons of pie,
And the turtles just shout, "We'll eat it by and by!"

Ripples tickle the grand river's sway,
As fishes tell tales of a daring ballet.
A whimsical race, where no one keeps score,
In this playful realm, who could ask for more?

A Cascade of Brilliance

A stream of mischief flows so bright,
It sparkles and laughs, what a sight!
Ducks in bowties dance along,
While fish hum a silly song.

Splashing around with joyous cheer,
Pigs in sunglasses, ever near.
They leap and twirl, no cares in sight,
Belly flops sparkle, what a delight!

A babbling brook, full of glee,
Tells jokes to the trees so free.
Squirrels chuckle, they can't hold it,
As water's pranks take a wild spin!

At twilight, when shadows are long,
The laughter echoes, a soft song.
Bubbles pop with a giggle sound,
As twilight's humor wraps around.

Echoes of a Sun-Drenched Shore

Waves burp and slosh with playful grins,
Sandcastles topple, oh, grand wins!
Crabs in party hats scuttle along,
As tide pools host a sing-along.

Seagulls squawk in a comical way,
Critiquing the surfers who sway.
"Not quite right!" they squawk and dive,
But fish just giggle, feeling alive.

Sunbathers slyly try to tan,
But end up looking like a ham!
With lotion smeared in a wild mess,
They laugh at their sun-kissed excess.

At dusk, the beach parties with flair,
Dance-offs with seashells in the air.
Mermaids join with fins all aglow,
Echoing laughter where breezes blow.

The Allure of Amber Waves

Fields of honey, a sticky delight,
Bees wear fedoras, quite the sight!
They buzz a tune, oh so dandy,
While flowers sway, feeling quite randy.

A picnic planned with treats galore,
Sandwiches wobble, what a chore!
Ants throw a feast, oh what a tease,
Trying to sneak a crumb or three.

Kites once flown, make friends with trees,
Caught in branches, swaying with ease.
Kids laugh out loud, they're on a quest,
For the grand prize of a kite that's best.

As evening sets, the glow gets bright,
Fireflies twinkle, oh what a sight.
S'mores in hand and laughter near,
Happiness shines, that much is clear.

Serenity in Shimmering Hues

A lake reflects the silliest things,
Fish with hats, and frogs that sing.
They throw a bash on a lilypad,
While turtles grin, oh how they're glad.

Boats that giggle on rippling waves,
Dance to the rhythm of nature's braves.
Skimmers race, trying hard to win,
While ducks cheer loud, "Let the fun begin!"

Clouds take form in laughter's disguise,
Winking at sun and sparkling skies.
A wind that tickles the grassy shore,
Echoes of laughter, who could want more?

As night approaches, laughter does rise,
Fireflies flash like tiny fireflies.
A party of nature, with friends so true,
In shimmering hues, their joy anew.

Waves of Eternal Luster

A fish in shades of yellow, tightrope on a wave,
Says, 'Catch me if you can!' while doing a brave save.
The crabs start to tango, a spectacle to see,
As they dance on the shoreline, both wild and free.

The seagulls squawk in laughter, no time for a nap,
While a dolphin makes a splash, with a cheeky clap.
A beach ball's flying high, a pass with a twist,
As everyone on the shore can't help but assist.

The tide rolls in with giggles, a game of tag ensues,
Building castles from the sand, facing awkward blues.
A sunburned pair is laughing, with sunscreen left unscathed,
They accidentally marked their faces—what a charade!

With waves of gold and laughter, they ride out with glee,
A perfect day of funny blunders, as happy as can be.

Harvesting the Sun's Embrace

Jellyfish in a smoothie, bright and full of zest,
Sips of ocean sunshine, their favorite quest.
The turtles roll their eyes, say, 'What a strange drink!'
While seahorses shake their tails—oh, what do we think?

Crabs in sun hats searching for the ultimate prize,
A treasure full of sunbeams, beneath the bright skies.
They dig with silly fervor, in a dance of delight,
With sandy snacks and laughter, the day feels so bright.

Fishermen tell tall tales, of catches that got away,
While octopuses chuckle, in their hilarious play.
'Did you catch the sun today? It slipped right through my net!'
With salty winds and glee, they've nothing to regret.

With waves that shimmer brightly, they ride into the dusk,

Harvesting the sun's joy, in laughter, we trust.

Flows of Liquid Joy

A river full of giggles that splashes come what may,
Ducklings playing poker, with cards made from clay.
The otters hold a contest, who's fastest on the float,
While fish tell silly stories, as they share their boat.

The sun sets in a wink, painting ripples gold,
As frogs croak crazy jokes, their humor never old.
With a splash and a slide, they create quite a scene,
The water tickles laughter—oh, where has it been?

Turtles use the current, for a lazy afternoon,
While beavers build a clubhouse, with a giant wooden spoon.
With waves of liquid joy, and silly splashes sweet,
Every drop a giggle, every turn a treat.

In this flowing laughter, the water sings a tune,
As the sun winks again, silver kisses from the moon.

The Gleam Beneath

A shimmering fish parade, they twirl and twinkle bright,
With costumes made of bubbles, they dance from day to night.
Starfish cheer them on, with claps that sound like cheer,
In this gleam beneath the surface, life's funny and near.

An eel with silly glasses dives deep for some fun,
While crabs hold an art show, painting shells on the run.
An octopus writes poems, with ink made of flair,
As jellyfish flash disco lights, in their colorful glare.

With sea slugs as the judges, they're critiquing the show,
Saying, 'That dance was great, but your wig was a no-go!'

As bubbles burst with laughter, and smiles start to swell,
In this gleam of hilarity, they've cast quite a spell.

So here beneath the surface, in laughter we bask,
In the gleam of life so silly, let's not stop to ask.

Sunlit Portals to Tranquility

In a boat made of cheese, we float with glee,
Chasing ducks dressed in suits with a key.
The sun wears sunglasses, so bright and bold,
While fish tell jokes about the great scold.

Penguins in swimsuits dance on the shore,
Sipping lemonade, they always want more.
With jellybeans raining from cotton-candy skies,
We laugh till we cry, oh what a surprise!

Glistening Pathways Underneath

Bubbles pop like popcorn in a fizzy stream,
Toads croak karaoke, living the dream.
The water's so slippery, we slide and glide,
On a banana boat, we joyfully ride.

Seagulls wearing hats sing tunes off-key,
While turtles play poker, just sniffing the tea.
Popcorn clouds drift by, oh what a treat,
We dance like fish with two left feet!

A Canvas of Radiant Motion

A canvas splashed with colors so bright,
Dancing jellyfish glow in the night.
With paint-covered crabs and brush-toting seals,
Artistic chaos, what fun it reveals!

The waves wear bowties, how posh and neat,
While octopuses juggle, oh such a feat!
A picnic on lily pads, oh what a spread,
On cookies and laughter, we all are fed!

Echoes of Effulgent Waters

Frogs hosting movies, a film by the bay,
With popcorn that hops right into the fray.
The stars like disco balls twinkle and sway,
A night full of giggles, what a humorous play!

Fireflies are dancers, they twirl in delight,
While raccoons play cards under soft moonlight.
From whispering waves, laughs bubble and bloom,
In this silly kingdom, we all share a room!

Sunlit Whispers

In the lake, my toe takes a dive,
Fish giggle, thinking I'm alive!
Splash splash, oh what a scene,
Ducks quack laughs, they're quite the keen.

With a wink, the sun threw a wink,
Off my head, the droplets clink!
A frog jumped in, poetry in motion,
Grinning wide, full of devotion.

The breeze tickles my cheek, oh what fun,
Chasing shadows, I dare to run!
Laughter echoes, the turtles cheer,
This is the best day of the year!

So here I splash, in cheerful glee,
Nature's jest, it tickles me!
A dance of joy upon the shore,
Who knew wet socks could mean so much more?

Glimmer on the Surface

A shiny fish shows off its bling,
Wobbling past with such a swing!
Chasing bubbles, it swirls and twirls,
While nearby, a snail hurls.

The sun takes a dip, has a laugh,
As I slip on my grassy path!
Giggles rise from the willow tree,
Waving leaves sing a melody.

Water shoes are far too tight,
Who needs style, when fun feels right?
Muddy feet, a badge of pride,
Watch me trip, the world's my slide!

A splash of joy, a sprinkle of cheer,
Swim like a noodle, or a silly deer!
With each ripple, life's a divine riddle,
Who knew silliness could be so middle?

Reflections of Radiance

Mirrored smiles on water's face,
Every splash, a silly race!
Reflections laugh, they can't stay still,
Jump in quick, it's a laughter thrill.

The dragonflies can hardly fly,
Turning flips, oh my oh my!
Swimmers shout, 'Look at me glide!'
Wobbling crabs break out in pride!

A tussle here, a tickle there,
Even the frogs are caught unaware!
A family of geese honk and play,
It's a riot on this sunny day!

With a splash of humor, life's a joy,
'Aha!' cries the fish, 'Catch me, boy!'
In this theatre, we twirl and sing,
Nature's comedy is the best thing!

The Dance of Dappled Light

Twinkling rays on the waves do prance,
Nature calls us to come and dance!
The beams jump in a silly swirl,
My shadow joins with a happy twirl.

The sun and I, we play a game,
Catching sparkles, it's all the same!
A bobbing hat, a splashing shoe,
Who knew wet fun could feel so new?

Laughter bubbles, a waterfall cheer,
As I dip my toes, all is clear!
With each ripple, joy is spun,
We're all just actors, playing in fun!

So let the light dance, let silliness reign,
In this frolic some time will gain!
Every giggle floats to the sky,
Under this sun, we truly fly!

A Serenade of Flowing Light

There once was a stream that danced with glee,
It tickled the toes of a curious bee.
The sun in its glory, a blushing sight,
Made fish wear sunglasses, oh what a delight!

A frog croaked a tune, quite out of key,
The otters rolled over, wild with esprit.
With splashes and laughter, a comical show,
They held a grand party, the river aglow!

A duck in a hat, he quacked with a grin,
Invited the turtles to join in the din.
A splash here, a dash there, such joy in the air,
While dragonflies danced, their wings all a-flair!

So come take a sip from this bubbly spring,
Where laughter and ripples are fit for a king.
For in every wave, there's a giggle or two,
A symphony bright, just waiting for you!

Cascades of Effulgence

In a babbling brook that sang of delight,
A snail wore a tie, oh what a sight!
He slid with a swagger, so proud and so slow,
Challenging the minnows, "I'm ready, let's go!"

The water cascaded, a mischievous spree,
While turtles debated, "Who's faster, you or me?"
They raced down the current, which led to a fall,
And tumbled like clowns, it was a splashy brawl!

A fish with a mustache, so dapper and fine,
Joked, "I'll teach you how to sip on pure brine!"
The frogs held their sides, they laughed till they cried,
As fish told tall tales of the big one that died!

So dip in your toes, let the ripples bring cheer,
To the humor that bubbles when nature's right here.
With giggles and splashes, let worries take flight,
In the splendid cascades of effulgent light!

A River of Radiant Memories

In a river that glimmers, oh such a bright flash,
The beavers are building a party, a bash.
With logs and some mud, they crafted a throne,
For an otter who claimed he was king of the bone!

They shared silly stories of fish that got away,
As they munched on some snacks made from river clay.
A heron flew by, dropping jokes from the sky,
"Why did the fish blush? It saw the net fly!"

The turtles all chuckled, their shells shaking too,
As they rolled on the banks, oh what a hullabaloo!
With bubbles and laughter, the moments were bright,
A memory made, within beams of pure light!

So gather your pals for a day by the stream,
Where laughter flows free, filling hearts with a dream.
From playful antics, come join in the fun,
A river of memories, smiles by the ton!

Echoes of Gilded Breezes

In the whispers of winds, you can hear them shout,
The frogs telling jokes, while the crickets all pout.
"Why did the lily refuse to bloom?" they did sing,
"It's saving its style for a royal spring fling!"

The shimmering air, it tickled pine trees,
While raccoons set traps for some late-night cheese.
They giggled and slid down the banks with a splash,
Playing tag with the waves, with each joyful crash!

The squirrels threw parties with acorns and nuts,
While finches crooned tunes, outsmarting the sluts.
With shenanigans plentiful, laughter was free,
Amid echoes of breezes, in total esprit!

So come you, dear friends, let the moments be bright,
With whimsy and wonder, we'll dance through the night.
For in every soft breeze, there's a hint of pure fun,
Creating a memory before day is done!

The Radiant Flow

In a stream where ducks wear hats,
And fish do dances with their spats,
The water twinkles like a grin,
As froggies leap and splash within.

A squirrel holds a fishing pole,
He reels in laughter, that's his goal,
The sun it winks, a cheeky sprite,
As bubbles pop with pure delight.

Chasing Sunbeams on the Surface

Beams of light skip like a stone,
While turtles chat on bubbles blown,
A crab in shades struts on the shore,
It's a beach party, who could ask for more?

Sandcastles wobble with a cheer,
As waves applaud, the coast is clear,
Fish play catch with jellybeans,
Life's a laugh in watery scenes.

Ethereal Streams of Liquid Light

A river flows with giggles bright,
Where otters slide with pure delight,
They wear tuxedos quite absurd,
And sing off-key, oh how they heard!

The waves are filled with tickles and tunes,
As frogs wear crowns and dance with spoons,
The currents swirl in great ballet,
Making even rocks want to sway.

A Tapestry of Luminous Currents

A rainbow slips on water's stage,
Fish throw glitter, it's all the rage,
While otters toast with seaweed snacks,
And turtles reply with silly quacks.

The tide brings joy, with laughter bestowed,
As seagulls play tag on the merry road,
Shells wear goggles for extra flair,
In this wild world of salty air.

Amber Hues of Nature's Caress

The river danced with jokes to tell,
Where two fish laughed, oh what the hell!
They flipped and flopped with gleeful glee,
One asked, "Is that a splash or me?"

Turtles wore their sun hats tight,
Sipping tea while taking flight.
A frog jumped high, lost its shoe,
And croaked, "Who knew? I'm not a kangaroo!"

The reeds stood tall, a raucous crew,
Tickling the breeze, as if they knew.
A heron tripped on slippery stones,
And managed but a few loud groans!

A beaver built a bridge for fun,
Guaranteed to be a water run!
With planks that wobbled side to side,
Its friends all cheered, "What a wild ride!"

Reflections of a Blazing Dawn

The sun peeked in, all bright and bold,
A cat replied, "Hey, don't be cold!"
With coffee cups full of bright ideas,
The birds chirped back, "Lighten your fears!"

A fish in sunglasses posed for snaps,
While ducks slid by in acrobatic flaps.
The ripples giggled, a ticklish sound,
As the sun bounced off, going around.

One squirrel leaped, a daring stunt,
Promised his buddies he'd never front.
He slipped on a leaf and fell with style,
The whole pond laughed, "That's worth our while!"

The lilies twirled in a morning sway,
Said, "Want to dance? Come out to play!"
And all the critters joined in the fun,
As dawn giggled on, another day begun!

Radiant Rift of Waters

A fish named Fred fancied a flair,
He donned a hat and a plaid square.
Wiggling his tail, he showed some class,
While others thought, "This guy's got sass!"

The crabs were cranking some tunes with beats,
They mixed it up with groovy feats.
The shrimp tapped claws, joined in the sound,
As seaweed swayed, proud and unbound.

A dolphin flipped and made a splash,
While octopuses giggled at his dash.
"Is it me or is today insane?"
Asked one, "It's just our crazy game!"

At dusk, the scene turned bright and loud,
The creatures swam, oh so proud.
With bubbles popping, laughter soared,
As day and night made their accord!

A Voyage Through Liquid Sunshine

With sails made from jellybeans and dreams,
A crew of clams plotted crafty schemes.
Their ship, a shell, was snazzy and bright,
As seagulls shouted, "What a sight!"

They raced the tide with giggles and glee,
While starfish shared jokes, just wait and see!
An octopus said, "I'll cook you a stew!"
As crabs danced around like a wild crew!

"Do you think we'll find treasure today?"
A brave little shrimp asked in dismay.
"Oh, we'll find treasure in each splash,
And who knows, a funny mishap might crash!"

So onward they sailed, with hearts so light,
Each wave brought laughter, pure delight.
Through puddles of joy and sunny sights,
They sailed to the end, oh what a night!

Secrets Beneath the Surface

Fish wear sunglasses, oh what a sight,
Bubbles of laughter, they float in delight.
Crabs throw a party, they dance with glee,
Under the seaweed, they live carefree.

Starfish play poker, no bluffing around,
While octopuses serve snacks they have found.
Jellyfish glow like lanterns at night,
Silly sea critters, what a weird fright!

Seashells whisper secrets, half under sand,
Conch shells debate, should we form a band?
Underwater giggles, echo so bright,
Their nautical antics bring pure delight.

When mermaids come near, the fish start to sing,
"Let's throw a bash, come join our fling!"
The tides roll in laughter, so carefree,
In this silly realm, we all wish to be!

Twilight's Shimmer

Dancing on waves like a playful ghost,
Sunset spills colors, it loves to boast.
Squids in tuxedos, they twirl and spin,
While starfish cheer, "Let the fun begin!"

The moon winks softly, a silver grin,
As dolphins are juggling—just look at them win!
Sea turtles surf on a bubbly crest,
Their laughter and joy, truly the best.

Seahorses gossip, tails all entwined,
"Did you hear that? It's the octopus kind!"
All critters come together, what a sight,
In shimmering waters, they dance through the night.

As twilight descends, the party is grand,
With a splash and a guffaw, they reach out a hand.
"Join us, dear human, don't just peep!
Dive into hilarity—come take a leap!"

A Cascade of Opulence

Rainbows cascade from waterfalls high,
While fish throw confetti and bubbles fly.
Noble crabs boast in their shimmering shells,
"Look at our kingdom, come hear our bells!"

Flamboyant flounders throw a grand ball,
With clams serving snacks, they're ready to enthrall.
Anemones dance in a luxurious flare,
Who knew that the ocean could hold such flair?

Eels in tuxedos parade down the way,
While plankton play maracas and sway.
With each splashing wave, a chorus will rise,
Under the surface, a feast for the eyes!

In luxurious splendor, the critters rejoice,
With laughter and mirth, let's all raise our voice!
For in these grand waters, both opulent and bright,
The joy of the sea is a marvelous sight!

Chromatic Ripples

A fish in a top hat swims past a seal,
Both giggle at ripples, what a strange deal!
The water is painted in hues so bright,
A carnival of color beneath the moonlight.

Pufferfish juggle, not puffed up at all,
While snails on scooters race down every hall.
Clownfish chuckle, their stripes all aglow,
In this underwater show, enjoy the flow!

The coral's a canvas, painted with flair,
As shrimp strut around, full of style and care.
With laughter like bubbles, they twirl and dive,
In a kaleidoscope world, where the sea comes alive.

In chromatic ripples, the fun never ends,
With tidbits of joy that the ocean sends.
So join in the splash, and let out a cheer,
For this wacky water world, so brilliantly clear!

Echoes of an Amber Stream

A fish wore a hat, quite bold,
Splashing around, feeling gold.
"I found a treasure!", he shouted loud,
As ducks stood by, utterly cowed.

The crabs held a dance, quite a sight,
In shimmering light, they grooved just right.
But when the sun set, oh what a mess,
They tripped on their claws, a true fishy stress.

A frog in a top hat joined the spree,
Jumping sideways with utmost glee.
He croaked out jokes that made all fish laugh,
While turtles rolled over, not needing a bath.

So if you wander where the sun glows,
You might find a party, as everybody knows.
Just watch your step, don't slip on a shell,
In this amber world, you'll be under its spell.

Where Sunbeams Dance

A bumblebee boogied, buzzing along,
Found a partner, a beetle so strong.
Together they twirled under the rays,
In a field of daisies, they spent their days.

Then came a ladybug, bright and round,
Joined the dance, whirling all around.
They laughed at the shadows, the grass beneath,
While the sun winked at them, just like a sheath.

But just then a breeze made them sway,
The bee flew off, quite far away.
The beetle called out, in a flickery trance,
"Hey! Come back! You were my sunbeam dance!"

As dusk painted hues, they bid adieu,
To the day's playful whimsy, a hullabaloo.
Tomorrow they'd meet, with fun to unveil,
Under the sun's glow, they'd dance without fail.

The Lure of Liquid Gold

A cat strolled by, tail held high,
Spotted a puddle that caught her eye.
"Is it gold?", she thought with glee,
But it splashed back, oh what a spree!

The puddle bubbled and laughed at her,
"You think I'm treasure? No way, dear fur!"
She licked her paw and made a face,
"You're just a mirage, not worth the chase."

A dog came trotting, tongue lolling wide,
Leapt right in, for a slippery slide.
"Look at me! I'm a dolphin today!"
He splashed gold everywhere, in pure play.

The cat rolled her eyes, and then she thought,
"Let's catch the sun, and give it a shot!"
With a leap and a bound, they cavorted about,
In laughter and joy, that's what it's about!

A Serpent of Radiance

A serpent slithered, all scales and shines,
With a silly grin and silly lines.
"Look at me, a great golden snake!"
He joked with a frog, who just couldn't take.

They draped in sunlight, took a break,
While the frog croaked puns for everyone's sake.
"Hey, snake, do you think you're divine?"
"Of course! I'm fabulous, just look at my shine!"

The fish all giggled, "What a sight to see,"
As the serpent posed near a grand oak tree.
He twisted and turned, in a dazzling flow,
"Watch me whirl! I'm the star of the show!"

As evening came in, with whispers so light,
They danced 'round the fire, hilariously bright.
For in the realm where laughter can sprout,
Even snakes can shimmer, without a doubt!

A Symphony of Shimmering Tides

In a lake where fishes wear hats,
There's a chorus of quacking chitchats.
The paddles go splish, the laughter so grand,
While turtles waltz, forming a band.

A duck with a bowtie is leading the show,
While seagulls do pratfalls, just look at them go!
Bubbles are bursting with giggles and cheer,
As the frogs in the reeds bring the crowd to sheer.

The catfish are juggling some cereal flake,
A catch of the day in a hearty light quake.
In this wetland, the splash flashes gold,
As stories of mischief and mayhem unfold.

So join in the fun, bring your flippers along,
In the merry brigade where all will belong.
For life is a rippling, bright jesting spree,
In the depths of the lake, come and dance with me!

The Treasure of Tranquil Depths

Beneath the calm, where the fish play hide,
A crab wears a crown for the royal tide.
Squid send silly messages in ink so bright,
While a clam takes a selfie, what a sight!

A treasure chest opens, and out jumps a cat,
Who claims that he's scuba diving, imagine that!
He's flinging seaweed like some sort of scarf,
And leaping with dolphins, oh what a laugh!

The eels are grooving, they've formed a conga,
While a starfish gives high-fives, such fun, oh my golly!
With pearls like marbles and a giggle parade,
Underwater antics are nothing but played.

So come seek your fortune in bubbles and glee,
For in these deep waters, you'll see all that's free.
With winks from the jellyfish, laughter abounds,
In this land of adventure, let joy know no bounds!

Dances of Light on Still Waters

The sun prances brightly on a mirrored expanse,
Where frogs in tuxedos are ready to dance.
They twirl with the lilies, they leap with a cheer,
While carp sing their hits with a splash for the ear.

A beaver's on maracas, a raccoon on drums,
They groove to the tunes, here comes the fun!
With dragonflies spinning in a fancy ballet,
It's a watery bash, hip-hip-hooray!

The otters are sliding, creating a fuss,
While turtles applaud with a slow, cheerful thrust.
With sparkles and giggles, the fish join the play,
As the day tiptoes softly and dances away.

So join in the riddle of ripples and light,
In this carnival, bubbling from morning to night.
With laughter and joy, the waters invite,
For the dance of the critters is pure delight!

Liquid Jewels in Nature's Embrace

In the woods where the puddles glimmer and shine,
The frogs wear monocles, sipping on brine.
With a splash of finesse, they leap near the muck,
While snails take a stroll, feeling quite pluck.

A heron in heels struts with such grace,
As bugs do the cha-cha, a wild little race.
A raccoon dons a cape, claims he's super fine,
Guarding shiny treasures—oh isn't that divine?

Each ripple a giggle, each droplet a smirk,
The critters conspire, oh what a quirky quirk!
With jewels of the earth dancing close by the shore,
Nature's own circus, a whimsical chore!

So dip in your toes, let the laughter unfold,
With gems in the water, a sight to behold.
In this fantastical realm, let your spirits fly,
For the joy of the liquid will make you feel high!

A Cresting Glow Amidst the Flow

A duck in a hat, so classy, he floats,
While fish wear sunglasses, with tiny brown boats.
They sip on sweet nectar, from leaves on the shore,
And giggle at frogs in a synchronized score.

The sun takes a dip, in a splash of bright cheer,
While crickets in bow ties beat drums with no fear.
With laughter like waves crashing high on the bank,
Even turtles dance, on the mud, proud and rank.

A pig in a tutu twirls close to the stream,
While snails find their rhythm, in a slow, sticky dream.
The breeze starts to whistle, a tune quite absurd,
As the cat takes a bow, but the dog just confers.

But as night takes the stage, the glow becomes sly,
The critters all gather, to watch fireworks fly.
And if you hear snickers from shadows nearby,
Just know it's a party, where laughter won't die.

Surfaces of the Ethereal Embrace

A floatsome of eggs, with a twinkling surprise,
Beckons along with sparkles that dance in the skies.
The crabs wear tall hats in a race with the tide,
While the seabirds critique from their perch, full of pride.

Each splash from a fish sends a giggle afloat,
As seaweed starts swaying, all nimble and quote.
The mermaids drop jokes that are cheesy and bright,
While orcas play chess in the shimmering light.

A clam with a pearl sings a tune from the deep,
While octopi juggle and whirl, not a peep.
They laugh at the barnacles glued to the rocks,
Who secretly envy their bright, flashy socks.

Yet when shadows grow longer, and humor does fade,
The playful find solace in a cool twilight parade.
As ripples keep dancing, with night's velvet guise,
All secrets are shared under twinkling, bright skies.

Shining Moments Under the Moon

Two owls in glasses share nuts under beams,
They plot an escape from the hunters' wild dreams.
With shadows of night weaving giggles and fun,
The woodland goes crazy until rise of the sun.

A firefly laughs in a luminous frown,
While squirrels throw acorns all over the town.
The grasshoppers join in, a ballet of sorts,
As raccoons play poker with marshmallow forts.

The stream hums a tune, all bubbly and sweet,
While frogs croak along to a rhythmical beat.
The bunnies hop hither, all giddy with cheer,
As night creatures gather, no reason to fear.

With moonbeams a-shimmer and mischief in air,
Each star becomes playful, and twinkles with flair.
And when dawn creeps in with a yawn and a sigh,
The world will be grinning, while waving goodbye.

The Sway of Soft Luminous Ripples

A fish in a dress spins around with delight,
Her friends all applaud in a fumble of fright.
The pond bubbles softly, with whispers of cheer,
As dragonflies joke, "We're the stars of the year!"

With laughter like bubbles that pop on the skin,
Each splash brings a giggle, the fun's about to begin.
The turtles line up for a belly flop game,
While the reeds sway together, all fancy and tame.

And when stars light the water, they poke at each wave,
An otter in sneakers shows off all his brave.
The night paints a canvas with dreams in the sky,
And everyone's dancing, as time flutters by.

Then in the cool stillness, mishaps they share,
With stories afloat, it's a grand circus fair.
And though dawn soon will greet with a yawning surprise,
Tonight's joyous shimmer brings laughter to eyes.

Sparkling Journeys

On a boat made of cheese, we sail,
Chasing fish with jelly in our trail.
With ducks in top hats, what a sight,
As we toast with lemonade every night.

Bubbles burst with giggles and cheer,
As we dance with a porcupine, oh dear!
We navigate waves of fizzy delight,
While seagulls perform in tutu's white.

We drop our anchor near a candy shore,
With gummy whales that make us roar.
Sailing through laughter, it's a blast,
The journey is funny, a joy unsurpassed.

Together we grin, no need to be wise,
For life's wild voyage is all about fries.
In this sparkling world, we play all day,
With all the funny hats we have on display.

Luminous Tides of Time

Once I met a clam with disco shoes,
He taught me all the groovy moves.
We danced on ripples, shining bright,
As fish joined in, what a glorious sight!

The lanternfish were quite the jest,
They juggled seaweed, truly the best.
With bubbles of laughter rising high,
Even the octopus couldn't deny.

Stars winked down, though some were shy,
A seal went cartwheeling through the sky.
Time slipped by in a splashy way,
As laughter painted the night from day.

We rode the waves of giggles and glee,
A tapestry of fun, come ride with me!
With luminous tides that never age,
Life's a funny story, turn the page!

Flowing Laughter of Cascading Light

The river flows with a fit and a giggle,
Tickling rocks, making them wiggle.
With frogs on surfboards, they all shout,
"Cannonball contest! Come check it out!"

Each splash echoes with chuckles and glee,
As snails race along, but they drink iced tea.
"Faster!" they yell, their shells all aglow,
In this race, well, it's slow motion, though!

A turtle pops up with a grin so wide,
As he slides down a waterfall for the ride.
The sunlight dances on rippling waves,
With giggles echoing through nature's caves.

Cascading light wraps around each cheer,
With dragonflies spinning, oh so near.
In this fun-filled flow, let's all unite,
For laughter's the treasure, shining so bright!

The Pulse of Gleaming Streams

In the bend of a river, turtles conspire,
Planning a party with chips and attire.
With water balloons and a slide made of mud,
They're all jumping in with a big thudding thud!

The fish form a band, all scales and fins,
Playing tunes that cause everyone grins.
While crabs flash their claws in wild display,
"Join us!" they say, "It's a fun, shellfish day!"

As raindrops tap dance, they start a parade,
With water-walkers in glam that they made.
Gleaming streams echo with giggles of glee,
This whimsical world is where we all agree.

So let's splash and swirl in the joyous rush,
In a laughter-filled current, there's never a hush.
The pulse of the stream sings a jolly tune,
As we dance with the fish under the bright smiling moon.

The Lure of Liquid Gold

At the edge of the brook, a fish did woof,
Trying to catch a snack, it slipped from the roof.
A splash and a flop, it danced with pure glee,
"Who knew that breakfast could swim here for free?"

As frogs all around croaked their ribbiting cheer,
Swimming lessons needed, but none would appear.
They jumped in the air, they landed with style,
Claiming that water was their favorite aisle.

The ducks formed a line, all oddly in sync,
Strutting their stuff like they were on the brink.
One quacked a joke, as the others did laugh,
"Who knew that wet feathers could be a great path?"

With bubbles and giggles, the waters did churn,
Each one causing laughter, their faces did burn.
So grab your floaties and join in the fun,
In this sparkly chaos, everyone's won!

Sun-Kissed Currents

A wave rolled up, with a gleam in its eye,
Whispering secrets as it waved goodbye.
"Catch me if you can!" it laughed with a splash,
While the surfers glided, they made quite the crash.

The sun shone bright, like a disco ball's glow,
Reflecting mischief as it danced on the flow.
Seagulls squawked tunes, a silly bird band,
Conducting their symphony on warm, golden sand.

A crab in a top hat strutted with flair,
Claiming that seaweed was quite the best hair.
While mollusks wore goggles, looking quite chic,
Wading through currents, not a hint of meek.

As children laughed loud, splashing water all round,
Water fights broke out, with giggles abound.
So grab your sunscreen, and let's make some waves,
In this humor-filled sea, let's be silly braves!

Reflections of Radiance

In the pond, a frog sang a top-ten tune,
Claiming he'd croaked it out by the light of the moon.
His friends all did chuckle, "Oh dear, what a sight!
A frog with delusions of pop-star delight!"

The fish swam in circles, gossiping fast,
"Did you hear about Harry? He's swimming at last!"
With gills that could flip, he danced with a spin,
"Look at me go! I'm the champion fin!"

The turtles, so slow, rolled their eyes with a sigh,
While plotting a race, under a noontime sky.
The winner, they said, would take all the brag,
But in end, as always, it was a slow drag.

With ripples that shimmered, the laughter did flow,
Unruly and silly, just like a light show.
So gather your pals, let the fun take its course,
In this radiant splendor, there's always a source!

Flowing Beneath the Glistening Sky

Beneath the wet sky, a dance of the falls,
Waterplay pranks echoing off canyon walls.
The otters were sliding, much to their delight,
"Who knew we could tumble with such graceful might?"

Splishes and splashes, the rhythm of joy,
While rafts made of leaves turned into a toy.
The fish joined the game, splashing about,
Creating a ruckus, without any doubt.

At dusk, the sun winked, casting shadows that pranced,\nEach wave told a joke, as if they all danced.
The riverbank giggled, with rocks rolling high,
As whispers of laughter cascaded nearby.

So sail down this stream, with friends all around,
In the laughter and joy, let your worries be drowned.
For flowing with humor, in nature's embrace,
Is the sweetest adventure, a most comical place!

www.ingramcontent.com/pod-product-compliance
Lightning Source LLC
Chambersburg PA
CBHW072124070526
44585CB00016B/1550